New Edition

DR. SEUSS

Gloria D. Miklowitz

DOMINIE PRESS

Pearson Learning Group

Publisher: Raymond Yuen
Editor: Bob Rowland
Designer: Greg DiGenti
Photo Credits: Bettmann/Corbis (pages 6, 20, and cover); J. Amos/Corbis (Page 16)

Text copyright © 2002 Gloria D. Miklowitz
New edition © 2004

All rights reserved. No part of this publication may be reproduced or transmitted in any form or by any means without permission in writing from the publisher. Reproduction of any part of this book, through photocopy, recording, or any electronic or mechanical retrieval system, without the written permission of the publisher, is an infringement of the copyright law.

Published by:

🔁 **Dominie Press, Inc.**
1949 Kellogg Avenue
Carlsbad, California 92008 USA
www.dominie.com

Paperback ISBN 0-7685-1217-4
Library Bound Edition ISBN 0-7685-1542-4
Printed in Singapore by PH Productions Pte Ltd
    5 6 PH 06 05

Table of Contents

Chapter 1
Feeling the Rhythm of Language....5

Chapter 2
Taking a Different Path 9

Chapter 3
The "Birth" of *Dr. Seuss*..................13

Chapter 4
Escape from Hollywood 17

Chapter 5
Contribution of a Lifetime 22

Glossary 26

Feeling the Rhythm of Language

Have you ever read *The Cat in the Hat, Horton Hatches the Egg, If I Ran the Zoo,* or *And To Think That I Saw It on Mulberry Street*? Those books, and many others, were written and illustrated by Theodor Geisel. You probably know him as Dr. Seuss.

*Dr. Seuss in front of the San Diego Museum,
which featured his artwork*

6

Theodor Seuss Geisel, called "Ted" by his friends, was born in Springfield, Massachusetts, on March 2, 1904. His grandparents had come from Germany. They built a brewery that produced some of the best beer in America. His father, Theodor, and his mother, Henrietta Seuss (called "Nettie"), settled close to Grandfather Seuss's brewery with their new son and two-year-old daughter.

When the young Dr. Seuss was growing up, his father tried to interest him in sports and hunting. But Theodor preferred going to the zoo and drawing pictures of the animals. One thing he learned from his father was, "Whatever you do, do it to perfection."

Nettie read to Theodor and his sister, Mamie, every night. She also soothed her children to sleep by chanting rhymes she remembered from her youth. Theodor loved the sound of words and said that he gained from his mother a feeling for the rhythm of language that later became part of his writing style. He enjoyed books so much that his mother often told him, "If you do well on your piano lessons, you can buy any book you want."

Growing up in Springfield made a lasting impression on Theodor. Years later, his memories of the town surfaced in his books, including the names of actual streets (like Mulberry Street) and the people he knew as a child. His images of Springfield include a look-alike of Mayor Fordis Parker on the reviewing stand in *And To Think That I Saw It on Mulberry Street.*

Chapter 2

Taking a Different Path

Even when Theodor was a child, there were clues pointing to the kind of person he would become. In school, he was playful, becoming the best ear wiggler of his friends.

Theodor was eleven when World

War I broke out. Germany torpedoed a British ship on which over a thousand people died, 128 of whom were Americans. Theodor's family had come from Germany and spoke German at home. Some Americans turned against Germans, especially when the United States entered the war in 1917. Classmates called Theodor "the German brewer's kid." The effects of the war put a social strain on the Geisel family. And in 1919 the passage of Prohibition, which made beer and other alcohol illegal, threatened the Geisel's livelihood. Their income depended entirely on the sale of beer.

When Theodor was in high school, his father insisted that he take fencing lessons. Theodor felt the lessons added nothing to his life. He signed up for an art class, instead. But when he worked on a picture upside down, his teacher told him that he would never succeed if he broke the rules.

Schoolwork didn't interest Theodor as much as drawing cartoons, writing humorous stories, acting in school plays, and becoming the "grind and joke" editor of the high school yearbook.

Theodor entered Dartmouth College in 1921 and quickly decided that he wanted to be the editor of the school's humor magazine, *Jack-O-Lantern*. Most of the students at Dartmouth called it *Jacko*. Theodor worked in the magazine office, sometimes staying up all night. A friend said that his humor was never mean. "He was a sweet man," he said. "He was always getting into trouble and laughing a lot. And he didn't study very well." Theodor intended to study. But instead, he found himself sketching weird animals in the margins of his notebooks while the teacher lectured.

In 1924, Theodor was named editor-in-chief of *Jacko*—the goal he had set for himself during his first year of college. The next year, he graduated from Dartmouth with a double major in English and writing.

Theodor wasn't sure how he would earn a living. He applied to Oxford University in England, hoping to earn a doctorate degree and teach English. But his life was about to take a different path.

Chapter 3

The "Birth" of *Dr. Seuss*

When Theodor enrolled at Oxford University, he was trying to please his father, who wanted him to become a college professor. But Theodor quickly felt "appallingly ignorant" among the other students. He preferred sketching rather than reading the required books.

One day, an American girl named Helen Marion Palmer stared over his shoulder as their professor discussed John Milton's epic poem *Paradise Lost*.

Instead of taking notes, Theodor was drawing an angel sliding down a sunbeam while oiling the beam from a can resembling a tuba. "You're crazy to want to be a professor," Helen said after the lecture. "What you really want to do is draw."

Theodor and Helen became good friends and soon fell in love. They traveled through parts of Europe on a motorcycle, went to parties with friends, and studied together.

Theodor left Oxford after one year and returned to Springfield. He hoped to make a living from his artwork. He submitted his cartoons to editors in

New York, but without success. Then he got a lucky break. The editor of *Judge*, the leading humor magazine in America at the time, published some of his cartoons and humorous articles. His first cartoon ran in October 1927. He signed it *Seuss* and added *Dr.* soon after, saying he deserved the honor for the doctorate he never got at Oxford. From that point on, he was known as Dr. Seuss. His cartoons also appeared in major magazines such as *Life*, *Vanity Fair*, and *Liberty*.

While working at *Judge*, Dr. Seuss continued to send cartoons to other magazines. One morning he received a letter from *The Saturday Evening Post*. It contained a check for $25 for a cartoon he'd sent them.

An even bigger break came when Dr. Seuss won an advertising contract for an insecticide called Flit. In one of

Dr. Seuss works at his desk with his wife, Helen

his cartoons for Flit, he drew a knight
in armor who was upset to find a
dragon on his bed. In the cartoon, the
knight says, "Darn it, another dragon.
And just after I sprayed the whole
castle with Flit!" Through that cartoon
and others for Flit, Dr. Seuss gained
national exposure. He coined the
phrase, "Quick, Henry, the Flit!" which
soon became a popular expression
across the country.

But Dr. Seuss's career in advertising
didn't last very long.

Chapter 4

Escape from Hollywood

Although Dr. Seuss and his wife could live well on his income from Flit cartoons, he wanted to do other things. He wrote an ABC book that featured a fictional, long-necked *whizzleworp*, but no publisher wanted it. In 1936, during a storm on a ship sailing to Europe, the rhythm of the engines caught Dr. Seuss's attention. He tried to think up words to match the steady beat of the engine parts and soon came up with *And to Think That I Saw It on Mulberry Street*, a book about a boy's walk home from school.

Twenty-seven publishers rejected the book before Vanguard Press bought it. It sold 10,000 copies at $1 each, and many millions more since then. Encouraged by reviews of *Mulberry Street*, Dr. Seuss began thinking of another children's book. An idea came to him on a train one morning. He wondered about the hat on the man seated in front of him. What if he threw the hat out the window? "The man would probably just grow another one and ignore me," he thought. From this musing came *The 500 Hats of Bartholomew Cubbins.*

Over the next two years he sold *The King's Stilts* and *Horton Hatches the Egg*. Children and adults in his growing ranks of fans looked forward to each new book.

On the approach of World War II, Dr. Seuss began submitting political cartoons to *PM* magazine, a liberal publication. He was too old for the draft, but he wanted to help the war effort. He and Helen moved to Hollywood, where he worked for movie director Frank Capra. There, he helped make training films for soldiers. Several of his films won awards. He won an Academy Award for *Hitler Lives* and another for a film on Japan. But he found working in Hollywood after the war "the worst experience of my life."

Dr. Seuss holds a toy character from one of his books, **The Cat in the Hat**

In 1948, Dr. Seuss and his wife bought a tower high up on a hill in La Jolla, California, and built rooms around it. He set up his office in the tower and worked there eight hours a day, seven days a week—longer, when the ideas flowed. If his ideas didn't flow, he'd lie on the floor and stare at the ceiling, or pace the floor. Helen became his editor and business manager, while writing her own children's books.

Chapter 5

Contribution of a Lifetime

When Dr. Seuss was asked by the Random House publishing company to write a Christmas story, he wrote the piece in one week. But it took him more than two months to find the right ending. The result was *How the Grinch*

Stole Christmas. Asked where the name *Grinch* came from, he said, "I just drew him and looked at him and it was obvious to me who he was."

In May 1954 *Life* magazine published a report on illiteracy among schoolchildren. That report prompted Dr. Seuss's publisher to give him a list of 223 words to use in an easy-to-read story for children. Dr. Seuss studied the list and found two words that rhymed. *The Cat in the Hat* became the first of his many fun-filled, easy-reading books. One of the books, which uses only fifty simple words, is *Green Eggs and Ham*. Once that book was in print, Dr. Seuss often had to eat green eggs and ham when he was invited to speak at conferences.

Dr. Seuss believed that his books had

to be funny. Humor, he believed, "is an important way of keeping the right outlook on the world." His wife, Helen, once said, "His mind has never grown up."

Helen's death in 1967 was a great loss for Dr. Seuss. She was his first love, his editor, and his business manager. But his lifestyle remained the same. He worked eight hours a day. When he was not writing, drawing, or gardening, he was reading. He read four or five books a week.

In his late 60s, Dr. Seuss became concerned about the damage being done to the environment. From this concern came *The Lorax* and later *The Butter Battle Book*, about the dangers of nuclear war.

At the time of his death on September 24, 1991, Dr. Seuss had written and illustrated forty-four children's books. His books had been translated into fifteen languages and sold more than 200 million copies around the world. Those books have inspired television specials, a Broadway musical, and a movie.

During his lifetime, Dr. Seuss won two Academy awards, two Emmy awards, a Peabody award, and a Pulitzer Prize for his lifetime contribution to children's literature.

When asked by a friend what message of wisdom he would like to leave to the world, Dr. Seuss said, "Whenever things go a bit sour in a job I'm doing, I always tell myself, 'You can do better than this.'"

Glossary

Appalling - surprisingly bad.

Brewery - a place where beer is made.

Director - a person who makes movies.

Doctorate - the highest college degree someone can achieve.

Fencing - a sport in which two opponents have a swordfight with protective gear and swords that are not harmful.

Hitler - the leader of Nazi Germany during World War II.

Ignorant - not having knowledge about something.

Lecture - a speech given by a college professor on a specific topic.

Literature - published writing.

Margins - the edges of a sheet of paper or a book.

Nuclear War - a war in which nuclear weapons are used. Nuclear weapons are many times more destructive than other kinds of weapons, and the land where nuclear weapons are used becomes harmful to human health for many years.

Outlook - the way someone views the world.

Oxford - the oldest university in England. It is about 800 years old and very prestigious.

Pulitzer Prize - one of the highest awards given to writers.

Torpedoed - attacked by a ship or submarine with a torpedo, a type of underwater missile.